Changing Chelmsford

Essex County Council

Site of the former livestock market in Victoria Road, 1831. On the edge of town and in the background is meadowland with the River Chelmer in the foreground.

Changing Chelmsford

John Marriage

Phillimore

1992

Published by
PHILLIMORE & CO. LTD.,
Shopwyke Hall, Chichester, Sussex

ISBN 0 85033 797 6

Printed and bound in Great Britain by
BIDDLES LTD.,
Guildford, Surrey

Dedicated to the memory of my parents,
Harry and Molly Marriage, who adopted
Chelmsford as their home town.

List of Illustrations

Frontispiece: Chelmsford, 1831

The Town Centre

1. The Shire Hall in the early 19th century
2. The High Street, *c.*1930
3. The High Street, *c.*1910
4. The town centre from St Mary's tower, *c.*1905
5. The town centre from St Mary's tower, *c.*1905
6. Tindal Street, *c.*1930
7. Tindal Square, *c.*1930
8. Tindal Street, *c.*1960
9. A. Driver & Sons, Tindal Street, *c.*1925
10. Duke Street, *c.*1910
11. Mr. Shedd's greengrocery in Duke Street in the 1930s
12. Moulsham Street, *c.*1938
13. The River Can in the 1930s

The Environs

14. Springfield Road and Horsepond Bridge, *c.*1900
15. Springfield Road, *c.*1915
16. Springfield Village, *c.*1905
17. Lawn Lane, Springfield, *c.*1910
18. Weight Road in 1898
19. Ploughing at Nabbotts Farm, Springfield in the 1950s
20. Ploughing at Nabbotts Farm in the 1950s
21. Fairfield Road, *c.*1900
22. Broomfield Road, *c.*1900
23. Rainsford Road, *c.*1905
24. Rainsford Road, *c.*1910
25. The Street, Boreham, *c.*1910
26. Danbury Hill, *c.*1900
27. Danbury Hill, *c.*1925
28. Broomfield Green in 1905
29. Ford End in 1926
30. Great Leighs, *c.*1915
31. Great Waltham
32. Little Waltham, *c.*1910
33. Leatherbottle Hill, Stock, *c.*1938
34. Graces Walk, *c.*1905
35. Harvest gathering, *c.*1915
36. Pleshey, *c.*1920
37. The post office at Roxwell in 1916
38. Skreens mansion, Roxwell, 1710
39. Link House Farm, West Hanningfield, 1930
40. Hanningfield reservoir in the late 1950s
41. View from Sandon Church tower, *c.*1920
42. Sandon post office in 1920
43. Writtle Green, *c.*1925
44. Weir Pond, Writtle Green
45. The Writtle to Chelmsford Road, *c.*1900
46. Woodham Ferrers, *c.*1930
47. Hylands House, Widford, *c.*1925
48. Chelmerton Lodge, Baddow Road, *c.*1900

Rivers and Open Spaces

49. Croxton Mill, Broomfield, in the 1950s
50. Little Waltham Mill, *c.*1900
51. Little Waltham Mill, *c.*1910
52. Canoeists on the River Chelmer, *c.*1950
53. The River Can, *c.*1900
54. The River Can, *c.*1905
55. The Stone Bridge across the River Can in 1945
56. The Stone Bridge, *c.*1913
57. Canoeist on the River Crouch
58. Canoeist on Barnes Millpond, *c.*1945
59. Canoeist by the Horsepond Bridge
60. Rowing boat by the Horsepond Bridge, *c.*1920
61. Writtle Swimming Club members, River Wid, *c.*1938
62. Bridge over the Gullet, *c.*1950
63. Barnes Mill Café and boathouse, *c.*1950
64. Paper Mills road bridge in 1927
65. Cuton Lock and Weir, Springfield, *c.*1950
66. Bell Mead, *c.*1950
67. The bandstand in the Recreation Ground, *c.*1900
68. Galleywood common, *c.*1900
69. Galleywood grandstand, *c.*1915

Commerce

70. Bond's store, High Street
71. Wenley's furniture shop, *c.*1910
72. The market, *c.*1910
73. Duffields solicitors, *c.*1938
74. Market Day in the 1920s
75. The Argentine Meat Company shop, High Street
76. Advertisement for H. & T. C. Godfrey, 1953
77. *White Hart Hotel*, Tindal Street, *c.*1910
78. *White Hart Hotel*, Tindal Street, *c.*1910
79. *The Griffin Hotel*, Danbury, *c.*1900

Acknowledgements

The author wishes to thank the following for permission to reproduce photographs: Jennifer Bailey, 11, 35, 126, 160; Eric Boesch, 40, 49, 52, 57, 59, 63, 65, 164, 165, 174; Chelmsford and Essex Museum, 118; Thomas Clarkson junior, 129, 167; Anthony St John Cramphorn, 64; Mrs. Peggy Double, 171, 172; Duffields, 73; Jon Ellis, 90, 91; Essex Record Office, 48, 50, 82, 84, 86, 99, 108, 127, 147, 149; Bill Holberton, 150, 153, 154; G.E.C. Marconi, 97, 98, 139, 140, 145; Vivian Marriage, 148; W. & H. Marriage & Sons Ltd., 100; Gwen Moore, 177, 178; Ken Nunn, 9, 117; Peter Relf, 123; W. G. Sawyer, 21, 176; S. J. Shipman, 60; Rob Tippler, 87-89, 105, 124; Barbara Trevor, 85, 125; Wenley & Bolingbroke Ltd., 71.

Preface

Chelmsford, county town of Essex, is one of the most rapidly growing communities in Europe, expanding as an office, electronics and retail centre as well as being home for thousands of London commuters.

From an ancient core situated at the junction of the River Chelmer and Can, the town this century has completely engulfed adjacent villages, whilst others, more distant, have become detached suburbs. Large tracts of farmland have disappeared under bricks and mortar.

In this book I have continued the theme established in my earlier book *Chelmsford – A Pictorial History*, which took a close look at the original small industrial and market town from Victorian times up to 1920. This book takes another look at the locality, moving forward to the 1950s and including wartime scenes. In those days, much of the traditional character of a market town with a rural hinterland survived. In the 1960s, the electrification of the railways and the increase of motor car ownership speeded the development of the district. Its good communications also encouraged the establishment of service industries and office development.

In 1974, local authority boundaries throughout England and Wales were revised. As part of these changes, the old Chelmsford Borough and Chelmsford Rural District were amalgamated to form the present district, almost reverting to the boundaries of the medieval Chelmsford Hundred. Thus, the present district has very ancient roots. There has always been a strong interdependence between the town and the surrounding villages and countryside. Modern communications have reinforced this historic bond and so I have thought it appropriate for this book to provide a record of the whole of the district – the current Borough of Chelmsford.

I have received considerable help and encouragement from very many people in the preparation of the book. In particular, I would like to thank Mrs. Barbara Trevor for information on Writtle, Mr. Jon Ellis on Crompton's and Mr. James Dunmow on Weight Road. Finally, I must again thank my wife who cheerfully corrected the grammatical and spelling errors and made invaluable suggestions on the contents.

Introduction

Chelmsford is a town with ancient origins. The Romans established a settlement in the Moulsham area, on their main London to Colchester route, close to the south side of the river Can. Most authorities now agree that it was called Caesaromagus, known to have been 28 to 31 Roman miles from London. After the Romans' departure, the town seems to have been abandoned. In Saxon times the main road was diverted through Writtle to avoid the dangerous Ceolmaer's ford – where earlier the more advanced Romans are thought to have erected a bridge crossing the Can and the Chelmer. Most of the population lived in the vicinity of Bishops Hall, whilst Moulsham, a separate village, developed south of the Can.

According to traditional belief Bishop Maurice bridged the Can around 1100, diverting traffic back to the old Roman route and away from Writtle. In 1199 the right to hold a market on the site of the present High Street was secured and the whole area was probably quickly marked out in plots as a planned village, with each plot-holder having a strip of land running down either to the Chelmer or the Can. A small trading town quickly developed, although totally different to the older agricultural community existing near Bishops Hall, and offering a variety of services to travellers along the road from London to Colchester, Ipswich and Norwich.

Although Writtle still had the larger population and remained the more important town for several hundred years, this little town steadily eroded Writtle's standing. As a result of competition from Chelmsford, Writtle's market, once the more significant of the two, closed by the 15th century. Moulsham soon became part of Chelmsford.

With its favourable position in the centre of Essex and surrounded by a diverse agricultural area, Chelmsford grew steadily, becoming the administrative centre for Essex and attracting industries such as tanneries, maltings and breweries.

In September 1888 the town received a Royal Charter to become a borough, its boundaries based on those of the original parish which had incorporated Moulsham. On the east side of the Chelmer, Springfield was excluded at its own request, together with Widford. However, later extensions to the borough chiselled away at Springfield, eventually claiming both its church and the green, as well as Widford, outlying parts of Writtle, and a small piece of the adjoining Broomfield parish. By the beginning of the Second World War the population of the borough was approximately 30,000, whilst the surrounding rural district had a further 30,000 people.

In 1974, there were major changes in local government structure and the Chelmsford borough and most of the surrounding rural district combined to form the borough of Chelmsford with a present population of about one hundred and fifty thousand. The main built-up area of the town has continued to grow outwards from its original nucleus centring on the High Street, and extends into Springfield and Great Baddow as a continuous urban area. There is also considerable development at Writtle and Broomfield. Other villages have greatly expanded and a new town has been established at South Woodham Ferrers, previously only a small community next to the river Crouch.

Although it has long since ceased to be a separate village, Moulsham Street – now a conservation area – survives with a strong local atmosphere. As a result of the freeing of the Mildmay entail, most of the 19th-century expansion of the town took place nearby, including the construction of New London Road. In the 1930s building work began on land that had once formed part of Moulsham Hall. At about the same time Princes Road, part of the first Chelmsford bypass, was opened and marked the limit of development. Strangely though, the council itself was the first to encourage building on the far side when it built Moulsham school, one of the most modern schools in the country. Unfortunately, it was totally isolated from residential development and for many years virtually all its pupils had to cross the busy bypass to gain access.

The construction of the terminus of the canal in Navigation Road led to the beginning of Springfield's expansion. Like Moulsham, major house building started in the 1930s with the construction of the Allied Housing Estate, consisting of 300 identical houses, close to the prison. However, sales were slow and, when the developers went into liquidation, the entire estate was purchased by the council. Post-war developments extended the built-up area northwards from the Green and eventually leapfrogged Chelmer Road (the first bypass) to devour arable land and create the so-called Chelmer Village.

William White described Great Baddow in 1848 as being one of the most handsome villages in Essex. However, since 1925 estates have been built on the farmland separating it from the town, though fortunately some of the attractive buildings in the High Street admired by White still survive. Sadly, they are now dominated by a 1960s high-rise shopping and residential complex. The nearby church, with its battlemented tower surmounted by a graceful spire, now occupies a lesser position. The churchyard, a meeting point for the Peasants' Revolt in 1381, is now a place of tranquility.

The Town Centre

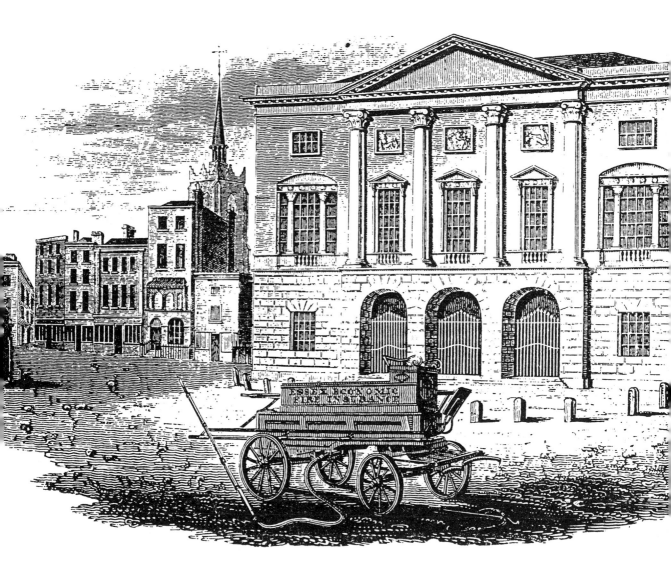

1. An artist's impression of the Shire Hall and adjacent buildings in the early 19th century. The Conduit stands in its original position in the centre of Conduit Square, now Tindal Square.

2.   The High Street, *c.*1930. The centre of a prosperous market and industrial town, then, as now, dominated by the Shire Hall, symbolising its important role as the county town of Essex.

3.   The High Street, *c.*1910, looking towards the major Springfield Road junction. The long established firms of Wenley and Bolingbrokes (now combined) were already entrenched on their present site. Opposite is Bond's, the town's first departmental store, famed throughout mid-Essex. In post-war years the latter was taken over by Debenham's and further expanded, but much of the facade remains.

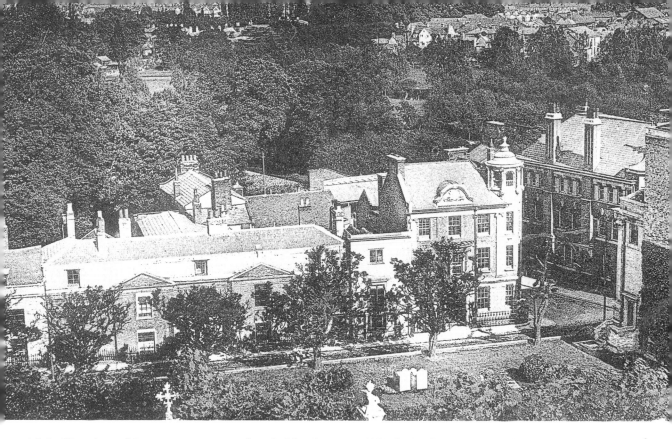

4 & 5. Two views of the town centre as seen from St Mary's tower, c.1905. In the view above, New Street and the Police Station can be seen with Springfield Road in the distance. Most of the trees have since been replaced by various buildings, including the Leisure Centre. The picture below shows Duke Street in the foreground and the railway embankment in the distance. The various properties between have since been replaced by the shopping precinct and County Hall.

6. Tindal Street, *c.*1930. The street was unique in supporting three adjoining public houses – the *Spotted Dog*, *The White Hart* and *The Bell* – whilst on the opposite side of the road was the *Market House*. All the inns relied to a great extent on the Friday market trade. Sadly, with the exception of the Market House, which is now an estate agent's office, all were demolished to make way for the present High Chelmer shopping precinct.

7. Tindal Square, *c.*1930. On the left-hand side of Market Road is the Corn Exchange, built in a neo-Renaissance style in 1857 by Fred Chancellor, the first Mayor of Chelmsford. On the right side is the Victorian-styled *Golden Lion* public house, with its curiously rounded elevations. The steel framework for the proposed first phase of County Hall can just be seen behind.

8. The photograph on the right shows the lower end of Tindal Street next to its junction with New London Road. The picture was taken a few years prior to the construction of the present shopping precinct in the 1960s. The shop with a Georgian bay window in the centre of the picture was the last of its kind in the town, whilst next to it is *The Dolphin*, another public house of character, alas, now gone.

9.   For many years A. Driver & Sons handled a large proportion of the printing requirements of the town. In this view, *c*.1925, two assistants pose in the entrance to the shop.

10. A quiet afternoon in Duke Street, *c*.1910, looking towards Tindal Square. The *Lion and Lamb* has since been replaced but most of the buildings on the right remain.

11. Mr. Shedd seen here standing in front of his greengrocer's shop in Duke Street in the 1930s. Greengrocers, by tradition, displayed their wares on the pavements, but freshness and quality were not impaired.

12. Moulsham Street looking towards the Stone Bridge, *c*.1938; in those days it was still a busy two-way road. The building on the right, just before J. A. Rankin, is the Regent, built in 1916 as a theatre but later used mainly as a cinema and now a bingo hall.

13. This 1930s view of the River Can, seen from the Stone Bridge, has totally changed in recent years. None of the buildings in the background, including Museum Terrace, now survive and most of the vegetation has gone. On the positive side, though, attractive riverside walks have been created on both banks and are greatly enjoyed by the public.

The Environs

Broomfield lies immediately to the north of Chelmsford town, astride the old Roman Road leading to Braintree and beyond. A hundred years ago green fields separated the village from the market town, with the exception of a few scattered houses. Today, the southern-most parts of the parish have already been engulfed by the town, both physically and politically. However, the main centre at Angel Green and Church Green still retains its village character. During the last war the village was host to an R.A.F. Air Operations Room which was based in a house near the church, thus continuing a long association with military aeroplanes. In the First World War the Royal Flying Corps established a landing strip near New Barn Lane. It was later used by light aircraft such as the one in which the Duke of Kent landed on his way to open the new bypass at Chelmsford on 25 May 1932. It has since fallen into disuse.

To the west of Chelmsford is Writtle, with which it now almost merges. It was formerly a Royal manor and, like the county town, has evidence of Roman occupation. In Saxon times it was a market town on the main London to Colchester road and was larger than Chelmsford. The market-house stood on St John's Green, next to the Saxon highway. The main highway was diverted back to its Roman route when Moulsham bridge was built at Chelmsford and Writtle gradually surrendered its importance. King John had a lodge nearby and hunted in the adjacent forests, part of which still survive at Highwood. The village later supported a number of rural industries including a large brewery and a mill, and it also had its own gasworks. More recently, and in conjunction with Chelmsford, it pioneered Radio communications. Writtle has retained the Great Green which is still bordered by a medieval church and many beautiful old houses. Apart from a large agricultural college, the village is now mainly residential.

Hylands House, a Grade II listed building, is accessible from the village. It was built in 1730 as a small red-brick early Georgian house, by Chief Justice Comyns Kt. It was later extended by subsequent owners to its present white stuccoed form, with the original red bricks being plastered over and the park enlarged. However, newer extensions have been removed by the borough council, who now own the house and the surrounding 440-acre park.

Roxwell was once part of the Manor of Writtle and later became a separate parish. During the 16th and 17th centuries a house at Skreens Park (now demolished) was at various times the home of a Lord Treasurer of England, a Lord Chief Justice, Sir Richard Weston (a leading poet of the age), Sir John Branston and Francis Quarles. Consequently, many influential figures of the time would have visited the village. However, the heart of the village is The Street, which still retains the form established over the centuries, despite some demolition and infilling. Many old buildings remain, including The Chequers and various cottages. Roxwell school, established as a National School, was erected at a cost of £500 in 1834 by Thomas William Branston of Skreens. Its opening was an instant success and five years later there were 73 boys and 84 girls on the school register – a remarkable number for such a small village.

It is arguable whether Galleywood is a village or merely a detached suburb of Chelmsford. The original community grew up around the crossing of the main London to Maldon turnpike with that of the Chelmsford to Tilbury route. Galleywood's main claim to fame was a racecourse built on the 175-acre common where racing took place regularly during the 18th century. The first recorded event was held in 1759 and a Queen's Royal Plate of 100 guineas was offered as prize money, the tradition continuing until 1876, while in 1770 George III also awarded 100 guineas. There were two racecourses: a straight one-mile course, and an oval course approximately two miles long which encircled a church (the only racecourse in the country to do so) and crossed the main road twice. In 1880, the course was redesigned, a new grandstand erected, and flat racing was replaced by steeple-chasing. Unfortunately, racing was discontinued in the late 1930s and the course became derelict. The grandstand, however, continued to be used for athletic meetings and social events, until it was demolished after the Second World War. In the 18th and 19th centuries Galleywood Common was also used as a training ground for the military, with soldiers marching there from barracks at Colchester and Warley. In some places traces of fortifications, built to defend London in the event of a Napoleonic invasion, can still be seen. Galleywood common is now used for informal recreation despite being reduced in size by the construction of Chelmsford bypass.

The three separate, but closely grouped, villages of Hanningfields – East, West and South – are today perhaps best known for the Hanningfield reservoir, built on farmland in the 1950s. The water is abstracted from the Rivers Stour and Chelmer and stored before being used for domestic and industrial purposes. The reservoir has become an important haven for wildlife. Danbury is situated on top of Danbury Hill, one of the highest locations in Essex. The heavily wooded ridge extends towards and includes much of Little Baddow before sloping sharply down into the Chelmer Valley. The Chelmsford to Maldon Road climbs steeply towards the shingled spire of the church, and was used by horse-drawn wagons to carry supplies from Maldon to Chelmsford prior to the construction of the canal.

Danbury is a popular residential area with much of the development hidden within wooded areas, thus maintaining a rural aspect. The National Trust, owner of the mainly gorse-covered Danbury Common and other land nearby, helps to conserve this heritage. Essex County Council also own land in the vicinity, including Danbury Park. Its lakes and beech walks, with their beautiful views of the surrounding countryside, are open to the public. Between Danbury and Chelmsford is Sandon, whose church and farm cottages are grouped prettily around a small green.

The parish of Woodham Ferrers includes both North and South Woodham, two places of total contrast. North Woodham is an attractive agricultural village situated on high ground, overlooking the Crouch valley. A minor road runs southwards through the village from Danbury. In contrast, South Woodham is located on flat land beside a road leading to an ancient ferry over the Crouch. When the railway track to Southminster was laid a few houses were built, and development continued earlier this century, when derelict farmland was sold in large plots, known as champagne sales. Unfortunately these plots were then developed with little or no thought for the eventual appearance of the area. Essex County Council has since redeveloped the site as a new town, and many of the residents commute to London.

The new town centre has been built in the form of a traditional Essex market town, but with limited success.

The original village of Boreham is situated near an old Roman road, and contains several 16th-century houses and a 14th-century church. Henry VIII built New Hall around 1518, and its visitors included both Mary Tudor and Elizabeth I. In 1943 the 16th-century façade, its entrance flanked by Doric columns surmounted by a metope frieze, was damaged by bombing, but fortunately has been restored. It is now a convent school.

The village of Pleshey, which had a castle in William the Conqueror's time, was the seat of Alfhers, High Constable of England. The castle was later occupied by succeeding Earls of Essex. After the deposition of Richard II, his half-brother, the Duke of Exeter, was seized by a mob and beheaded. Very little now remains of the castle, except for the massive earthworks, moats and a Tudor brick bridge over the inner moat. The village itself, however, is still contained within extensive embankments and a wide ditch approximately a mile in circumference. The original medieval street pattern, based on four entry points, remains unchanged.

Battlesbridge, at the extreme south of the borough, was once a bustling community for both travellers and traders. It was situated on the tidal head of the Crouch estuary up to the middle of this century and was a major centre for sailing barges. An important tide mill also stood there which inpounded the water at low tide.

Beside the old road to Tilbury and six miles south of Chelmsford the linear village of Stock is situated. It is built on high ground overlooking the River Wid, with a wide High Street containing a long green. The 14th-century church is remarkable for its timbered tower and spire, built upon a framework of huge beams. The only remaining windmill in the borough is owned and preserved by the Essex County Council. Its tower is of red brick with a wooden upper loft and it is one of the main sights of the village.

14. Springfield Road and the former Horsepond Bridge, c.1900. In 1943 the *Rosebery Temperance Hotel* and the shop next door were burnt to the ground after receiving a direct hit from an incendiary bomb. The site is now occupied by the Highbridge Road roundabout.

15.   Springfield Road at the junction with Navigation Road, *c.*1915, was a beautiful tree-lined avenue flanked by attractive houses, so different from today's busy commercial and heavily used road.

16.   Springfield Village, *c.*1905, was a small isolated hamlet at the upper end of Springfield Road. This view shows the *Plough* public house, which remains remarkably unchanged and is now well placed to serve the nearby housing estates.

17. Lawn Lane, Springfield, was a quiet tree-lined country lane until the post-war years. Dutch elm disease and development have swept away this once picturesque scene.

18. Frederic Weight, the landlord of the *Three Cups* public house, built Weight Road in 1898 on undeveloped land at the side and rear of the premises. The beautiful cast-iron railings in front of each house were removed during the war for the munitions drive.

19 & 20.   Ploughing and harrowing at Nabbotts Farm, Springfield, in the 1950s. Although mechanisation was beginning to take over, there was still work for the shire horses. Part of the North Springfield estate now stands on the land.

21. Fairfield Road at the turn of the century was a quiet and select residential street. The Eastern National Bus Station now occupies the land on the left of the picture, and a municipal car-park has been built on the right.

22. Broomfield Road corner, *c*.1900. Many of the buildings on the right-hand side of the picture remain, but the brick wall and trees opposite have been replaced by a row of shops.

23. This view at the junction of Rainsford Road and Rainsford Lane, *c.*1905, shows a well-ordered, peaceful scene. A major traffic junction now exists giving access to the town's gyratory system.

24. Rainsford Road, *c.*1910. The ornate front of the Pavilion was destroyed during the war and rebuilt in a simpler style, but the *County Hotel* is little changed.

25.   The Street at Boreham, *c*.1910. It still remains substantially unchanged, although the village has considerably expanded.

26.   In the days of horse-drawn vehicles Danbury Hill provided a long haul and a challenge to both horse and rider. No highway code was needed for these children, who had little to fear from the slow moving carts.

27. Another view of the long climb at Danbury Hill, *c*.1925. In those days it was still a major test for motor traffic, with probably much use being made of bottom gear. Today, the hill is of no consequence to modern cars.

28. Broomfield Green as it appeared in 1905. Then, as now, the *Angel Inn* was a popular venue on the way to Braintree.

29. This attractive thatched cottage at Ford End, seen here in 1926, has changed little today. Written on the reverse side of the postcard are the words, 'I think you may like to see this view of the cottage. Flowers are lovely'.

30. The main Chelmsford to Braintree road at Great Leighs, c.1915. The postcard was sent by a Great Leighs soldier to his girlfriend, in service at Beccles, relating his bicycle ride to Braintree. In those days cycling was the most popular form of transport.

GT. WALTHAM FROM CHURCH TOWER. 1964.

31. Great Waltham church stands at the very heart of the village, with ancient timber-framed and plastered cottages on three sides. This unusual picture was taken from the church's tower, looking towards the village hall.

32. This view shows the original village of Little Waltham, c.1910, strung along the main Braintree road. Many picturesque cottages flank the High Street, which has now returned to the more peaceful atmosphere of yesteryear, thanks to the construction of a bypass.

33. Leatherbottle Hill, Stock, c.1938, on the Chelmsford to Downham road. Its name is derived from a former public house which was situated nearby.

34. The entrance to Graces Walk, from Little Baddow Road, *c*.1905. Although somewhat altered today, it is still a local beauty spot. The National Trust owns much of the land in the vicinity. The message on the back of the postcard says, 'Don't you think this is very pretty. We went to it last Wednesday and it rained the whole day like the very deuce'.

35. During both world wars, most able-bodied men were away in the forces and women tackled many of their jobs. School children also did their bit and often gathered in the harvest. In this picture, *c*.1915, pupils of Margaretting school can be seen lifting potatoes, supervised by their teachers, Miss Hughes and Miss Batt.

36. Pleshey village, *c.*1920, was once one of the most important towns in England. Although only a few miles from the bustling county town, the village has changed little and still remains peaceful and quiet.

37. The post office at Roxwell in 1916. The postman prepares to start his rounds, whilst some of the bystanders seem more concerned with watching the photographer.

38. Seen here around 1910, Skreens at Roxwell was a large stately mansion built by the local landowner, Thomas Branston. It was enlarged by his successors but sadly was demolished earlier this century, although the beautiful encompassing parkland remains.

39. In pre-war days many Essex farmers were impoverished, their fields derelict or under used, the result of the nation's reliance on cheap foreign food. It was not until home production was promoted during the war that conditions improved. In 1930, Link House Farm, West Hanningfield, like so many farms, was just managing to survive, with outbuildings urgently needing repairs.

40. Hanningfield reservoir, seen here shortly after it was completed in the late 1950s. Acres of arable farmland and dozens of dwellings, including Fremnells, a lovely medieval house, were submerged. Presenting a raw appearance at first, the reservoir has now matured, helped by dense planting around the perimeter. This huge expanse of water is now an important wintering area for migrant water fowl and other birds.

41. Looking east from Sandon Church tower, *c.*1920. In the foreground houses are grouped around the village green, whilst snaking away into the distance is the Danbury road.

42. As a small village Sandon has never boasted a wide selection of shops. In 1920 the post office, on the Danbury road, also served as a general store, where the proprietor, A. F. Gould, was ready to sell most day-to-day items, accompanied no doubt by a friendly chat.

43. This bird's-eye view showing Writtle Green was taken about 1925. It is reputedly one of the largest village greens in Essex, with a fine range of attractive houses of varying ages and designs surrounding it. The Green is a popular venue for fêtes, fairs, cricket matches and other outdoor functions throughout the year, and plays an important part in village life.

44.   At the east end of Writtle Green is Weir Pond. Although once a watering place for passing animals, it is now home to ornamental ducks and geese.

45.   In the early 1900s the main Writtle to Chelmsford Road was a quiet and shady macadamed highway with little passing traffic. Today, the same road is busy with cars and buses. Sadly, the huge elms have gone, creating a more open aspect.

46. Woodham Ferrers, at the extreme east of the present district, remains a quiet rural village, unlike the neighbouring South Woodham. The two villages are united in the same parish, the latter being developed haphazardly at the turn of the century and expanded by the Essex County Council as a planned new town.

47. Hylands House, Widford, *c.*1925, was owned by Mr. Hanbury of the well-known brewing family and his wife. The central portion of the house was built in 1730 and extended by successive owners until it was acquired by Chelmsford Council in 1966. In 1989 the Victorian extensions on the first and second floors, together with the impressive porte-cochere, were demolished, and the building returned to its early 19th-century form.

48. Chelmerton Lodge, Baddow Road, *c.*1900, was an attractive Victorian house, which originally backed on to open fields and the Chelmer Valley. It has been substantially altered and today it would be quite impossible for the children to play with their hoops in the busy road.

Rivers and Open Spaces

Rivers and watercourses have always had a great impact on the whole of the Chelmsford district, both in terms of utility and landscape. Geographically, watercourses quarter the district and take the form of an irregular cross, with land sloping gently down from all sides. The largest, and one of the longest rivers in East Anglia, is the River Chelmer which enters the extreme north of the district near Ford End and flows southerly to Chelmsford where it turns eastwards, uniting with the River Can, which rises near Good Easter in the west of the district. Prior to merging with the Chelmer, the Can receives water from the River Wid, a small stream which enters the district from the south near Stock. From Chelmsford, the Chelmer continues eastwards until it flows into the Blackwater Estuary at Maldon.

Watermills have existed at intervals along all these rivers. Most ground corn into flour, although at Little Baddow paper was produced. The water was impounded at each mill by a weir in order to provide a good head of water with which to turn the mill wheels. Mills were built in various shapes and sizes ranging from modest structures like those at Roxwell and Widford to substantial buildings such as Moulsham mill. In summer, the mill ponds were popular with the locals who used them as rudimentary swimming pools, with makeshift diving boards. Lower down, the locks were also popular for swimming and diving, though it has never been advisable to swallow the water! In some places, like Writtle, changing huts were provided and a swimming club was organised. Fishing was another pastime. Today, despite the demise of the industry, some mill buildings have taken on a new role. Springfield mill, in Victoria Road, a magnificent white painted weatherboarded structure, has been converted and is now a popular restaurant, whilst Croxton's mill at Broomfield has become a private residence.

Upstream from the centre of Chelmsford the water levels maintained for the millers have in many places been lowered, resulting in adverse changes to the landscape. Downstream from Chelmsford, on the right to the tidal estuary, the traditional water levels have been retained and the wide pastoral valley mostly preserves its age-old appearance. This is due in no small part to the existence of the Chelmer and Blackwater Navigation, dug in 1796 when the old river was converted into a navigable waterway. The conversion was achieved by widening, straightening and deepening the river channel and constructing 13 locks along the route. Although built primarily to convey goods and materials between Heybridge Basin and Chelmsford it was also used to carry goods to and from the various village wharves and mills.

The cargo-vessels were flat-bottomed wooden lighters 60 ft. by 16 ft., with a draft of two feet and were horse-drawn until about 1950. Motorised steel barges were subsequently introduced and used for nearly twenty years. Commercial cargo traffic has now ceased and the canal is used purely for recreational purposes, with boaters and anglers enjoying water pursuits and ramblers using the old towpath, now a public right of way. Water is discreetly abstracted for local use and irrigation purposes whilst willows grown on the banks of the river are used in the making of cricket bats. The Company of Proprietors of the Chelmer and Blackwater Navigation Ltd., who originally petitioned Parliament in 1793 for building permission, are still the owners. The entire canal has recently been declared a conservation area.

49. Croxton Mill, Broomfield photographed in the 1950s, shortly after it ceased to be used commercially. In summer, the mill pond was used by the locals as a swimming pool. The mill, much altered, is now a private house.

50. Little Waltham Mill, *c.*1900, was a busy and attractive structure near to the village.

51. The same mill, *c.*1910, fell victim to competition from the newly built and more efficient steam roller mills. Today, only a weir marks the site.

52. A small group of paddlers prepares to canoe down the River Chelmer from Little Waltham, *c.*1950.

53. The River Can near Seymour Street, c.1900. The Recreation Ground (now Central Park) was already in existence on the left bank but the other side was still farmland. It is now occupied by the Falcon Bowling Club, the Football Club and the Essex Cricket Club.

54. Rowing down the River Can towards the New London Road bridge c.1905. Sadly, Museum Terrace on the left, and other buildings were all demolished in the 1960s but on the positive side, Central Park has been extended up to the bridge.

55. The Stone Bridge, built across the River Can in 1787, remains an elegant feature of the town. In 1945 the adjacent banks still had a rural appearance but this was lost in the 1960s when two concrete banks were built as part of a flood prevention scheme.

56. Another view of the Stone Bridge, c.1913. The adjacent Methodist church was demolished in the 1960s to make way for an extremely ugly block of shops and high rise offices and unfortunately the beautiful tree was also lost.

57.	The River Crouch forms the southern boundary of the district. Battlesbridge, at the tidal head, and was once an important local port that boasted a thriving tide mill. In its heyday as a port it was the custom to moor craft in the pond, pictured here, to escape the tide. In 1950, the tidal gates giving access to the mill pond were still complete and could be navigated with care.

58.	Immediately after the war, many young people were introduced to canoeing by the acquisition of United States Army Airforce war surplus long range fuel tanks. Acquired from the local dump for a small fee, they were converted into rudimentary, if somewhat dangerous, canoes. This young paddler takes his dog for a trip in Barnes Millpond, c.1945.

59.	The author seen here emerging from under the Horsepond Bridge. The land in the foreground is now part of Tesco's store.

60. A rowing boat by the Horsepond Bridge in Springfield Road, *c.*1920. The Horsepond was part of a narrow alternative channel of the Chelmer which rejoined the main course below Springfield Road Bridge. It was infilled in the 1960s.

61. Swimming galas were regularly held on the River Wid, which until 1939 had been the home of the Writtle Swimming Club. Members were expected to be proficient swimmers and lessons took place under the guidance of Corky Thornitt.

62. This little bridge, pictured here in 1950, provided access to Kings Head Meadow from Springfield Road and once spanned The Gullet, a narrow connecting channel between the River Can and the Chelmer. It was infilled in the 1960s as part of a flood prevention scheme.

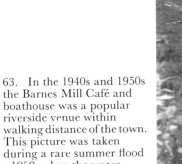

63. In the 1940s and 1950s the Barnes Mill Café and boathouse was a popular riverside venue within walking distance of the town. This picture was taken during a rare summer flood c.1950, when the water reached the boathouse.

64. A sketch of the original Paper Mills road bridge over the River Chelmer at Little Baddow. It was built in 1797, to a design by John Rennie, the famous civil engineer. Its abutments were of brick with a central span of timber. By the 1930s it had become unsafe and was replaced by the present concrete structure.

65. Cuton Lock and Weir, Springfield, *c.*1950, complete with wartime pill box. It was then a quiet and remote spot far from busy thoroughfares and crowds. Today, its tranquility is lost for ever as unending traffic on Chelmsford bypass thunders past, less than 100 yards away.

66. Bell Mead, *c.*1950, was an attractive municipal garden area, with a South African War memorial as its central feature. Part of the gardens still remain, together with the memorial, but the Bellmead Service Road now occupies part of the site.

67. The old bandstand in the recreation ground was a popular venue, *c.*1900, and visiting bands provided a restful Sunday afternoon's entertainment for the townsfolk. It was badly damaged during the last war when the nearby drill hall received a direct hit, and was demolished soon after.

68 & 69. Flat racing was first held at Galleywood in 1759 but in 1880 a steeplechase course was laid out and a new stand built. In the 1930s the legendary Golden Miller owned by Miss Dorothy Paget won here. The view on the left shows the course from the grandstand as it was at the turn of the century, and during the Great War the Army requisitioned the stand for accommodation as the picture below shows.

Commerce

Chelmsford High Street has been the centre for trade and commerce since its beginnings in the 13th century. It was later supplemented by premises in Moulsham Street, Tindal Street and to a lesser extent by Duke Steet. Some of the best known shops in the Victorian and Edwardian eras were Bond's, Wenley, Bolingbroke, Grippers, Luckin Smith and Clarkes, all owned by local entrepreneurs. Banking also became established about this time, the oldest being Barclays Bank which absorbed the Essex Bank, founded in Chelmsford in 1801 by Crowe, Sparrow and Brown. Like so many old market towns, Chelmsford had a wealth of public houses, most of which were to be found in the main streets, but with the advent of home entertainment in the post-war years many of them were forced to close.

As one of the larger villages, Writtle had, until recently, an important and flourishing shopping facility. It included local favourites such as Green and Sons the butcher's, whose owner farmed Montpeliers Farm, E. W. Lodge the baker's, and Fairhead the grocer's. Sadly, due to competition from Chelmsford's much larger retail centre, the range and number of shops are now much reduced, a trait shared by other neighbouring villages. At Great Baddow, where many of the traditional shops along High Street have disappeared, a new shopping centre has been created, the style of which reflects the suburban character of new housing in the vicinity.

70. Bond's was formerly Chelmsford's most successful High Street store and famous throughout the district. From small beginnings it gradually engulfed the adjoining premises. The once separate properties can clearly be seen above fascia level. Debenham's now occupy the site.

71. Originally a private house, this photograph shows Wenley and Son, c.1910. The family lived above the converted ground floor furniture shop, until the building was destroyed by fire in the 1950s. The Bolingbroke & Wenley successor firm still occupies the site.

72. Chelmsford stall market, c.1910, was situated on the corner of Market Road and Threadneedle Street from 1880 until the middle of this century. Today, the market is held under the multi-storey car-park and the tradition of supplying cheap fresh fruit and vegetables continues.

73. Many High Street properties had been converted from private houses. This picture, *c*.1938, shows the only remaining unaltered building which has been occupied for many years by Duffields, a long established firm of family solicitors.

74.   Market Day in Chelmsford was always extremely busy. During the 1920s, Essex farmers sold their meat next to the cattle market and judging from the photograph the meat was obviously very popular and probably quite cheap.

75. Between the wars the Argentine Meat Company, later the London Central Meat Company, in the High Street, provided good quality meat at moderate prices. It subsequently became a branch of Dewhurst's.

76. H. & T. C. Godfrey were very well known in the district. Their shop specialised in saddlery and travel goods, and most outdoor summer events depended on them for the provision of marquees and other fête equipment. This advertisement appeared in 1953. They closed in the 1980s.

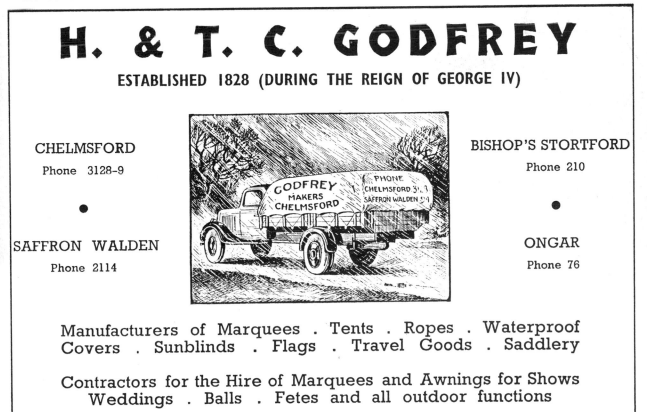

H. & T. C. GODFREY

ESTABLISHED 1828 (DURING THE REIGN OF GEORGE IV)

CHELMSFORD

Phone 3128-9

•

SAFFRON WALDEN

Phone 2114

BISHOP'S STORTFORD

Phone 210

•

ONGAR

Phone 76

Manufacturers of Marquees . Tents . Ropes . Waterproof Covers . Sunblinds . Flags . Travel Goods . Saddlery

Contractors for the Hire of Marquees and Awnings for Shows Weddings . Balls . Fetes and all outdoor functions

77 & 78. The *White Hart Hotel*, Tindal Street, *c*.1910, was one of the oldest and best known hotels in Chelmsford until its demolition in the 1960s. Extensive stables and garaging at the rear were reached by a tunnel entrance from the street.

79. The *Griffin Hotel*, seen here *c.*1900, was situated almost at the top of Danbury Hill, and has always been a welcome sight for the thirsty traveller, particularly after the long haul up from Sandon. Outwardly it remains unchanged.

80. Prior to the growth of home entertainment, most people went to the pictures at least once a week. From the late 1930s through to the early 1960s, Chelmsford had four cinemas, each showing weekly programmes. Their programmes for the week starting Monday 14 December 1953 are shown here.

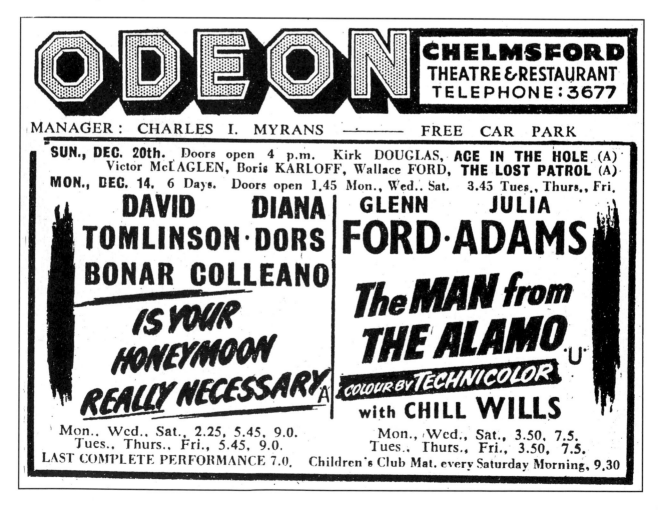

Industry

Industry grew up around Springfield Basin, and included the first inland gasworks in the country. The railway, built in 1843 from London to Colchester, attracted various firms which established themselves next to the goods yard. Towards the end of the 19th century the Crompton, Hoffmann and Marconi factories were founded and together they employed hundreds of workers, many of whom cycled in daily from as far afield as Danbury, Great Waltham and Galleywood. Unfortunately, of the three factories only G.E.C. Marconi survives, but it has expanded and now produces a wide range of electronic products at various sites in the town and adjacent villages. Other firms have come and gone, including Clarkson Ltd. (bus manufacturers), Coleman and Morton (agricultural machinery specialists) and Eddington & Stevenson, manufacturers of traction engines and other contracting equipment. Less well known is the growth of the soft drinks industry, such as Britvic Soft Drinks plc. which has expanded from small beginnings in Cottage Place into a major national concern.

81. Barnes Mill, a very attractive white-painted weatherboarded structure, was a large watermill serving Springfield. This picture was taken in 1946 when it had just ceased to be used regularly for grinding corn. It has since been converted into a private house.

82.   Water mills were spaced regularly every mile or so along the Chelmer. This photograph, *c.*1900, shows Little Baddow
Mill whose flour was sent down the canal to London. Sadly, like so many mills, it was destroyed by fire many years ago
and only a portion of the mill house remains.

83. Collecting straw the traditional way from the fields at Nabbotts Farm, Springfield, in the late 1940s. The use of horses and carts on farms was then still common and hence there was still a good market for straw, unlike today.

84. Before farm mechanisation, many workers were needed to gather the harvest, and wives and children were expected to join in. This picture was taken at Greys Farm, Chignal Smealy in Victorian times. The farm bailiff, with shotgun at the ready, stands prepared to bag any rabbit which might appear from the last cut.

85. Harcourt Pamplin (centre) with his assistant Harry Brown working at Writtle Forge, St. John's Green, *c.*1935.

86.   Brown and Sons workshop, seen here in the early 1900s, were the main timber merchants in the area. They imported timber via the canal, whilst hardwoods were purchased locally as standing timber.

87, 88 & 89. At the turn of the century, Munnion and Sons had a substantial coach and carriage works in Springfield Road. Initially, work was confined to turning out the ubiquitous horse-drawn carriage, but later they produced the bodywork for most of Clarkson's Steam Buses and for early car manufacturers, like Bentall's of Maldon. The firm later moved to Great Baddows, where they remained in business until the second half of the century.

90.   Crompton's (later Crompton Parkinson Ltd.) established their factory at Writtle Road in 1885 and soon created an international reputation for quality electrical engineering. Sadly, the factory closed in the 1960s and production moved elsewhere. The huge traction motor assembly shop is shown here, about 1950.

91.   Christmas Eve 1948. Draughtsmen and tracers from Crompton Parkinsons Ltd., gather cheerfully in the machine drawing office for this group photograph, including the Chief Draughtsman, Frank Perry, sixth from the left. In those days decorations were put up only for the Christmas Party and removed immediately afterwards.

92.   Hoffmann's works, c.1915. Large numbers of women were employed on quality control and were kept busy throughout both world wars.

93. The jig and tool drawing office at Hoffmanns, about 1950. Women were employed as tracers, refining and developing the technical drawings prepared by draughtsmen.

94. Hoffmanns' bearing production was surprisingly complex. This extract from a sales brochure, c.1950, shows a product that was used in railway engines and rolling stock all over the world.

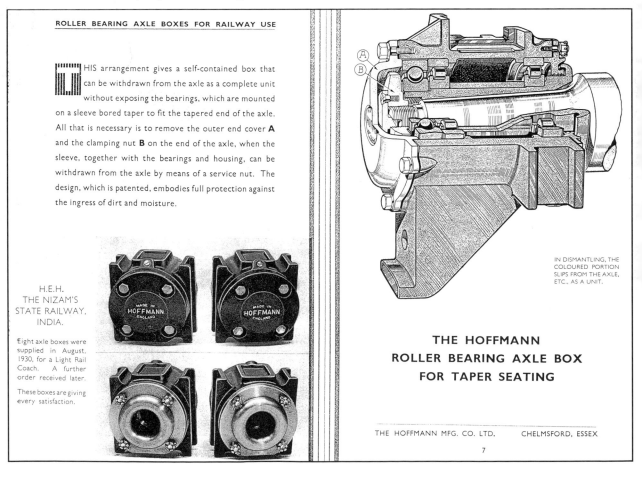

ROLLER BEARING AXLE BOXES FOR RAILWAY USE

THIS arrangement gives a self-contained box that can be withdrawn from the axle as a complete unit without exposing the bearings, which are mounted on a sleeve bored taper to fit the tapered end of the axle. All that is necessary is to remove the outer end cover **A** and the clamping nut **B** on the end of the axle, when the sleeve, together with the bearings and housing, can be withdrawn from the axle by means of a service nut. The design, which is patented, embodies full protection against the ingress of dirt and moisture.

IN DISMANTLING, THE COLOURED PORTION SLIPS FROM THE AXLE, ETC., AS A UNIT.

H.E.H.
THE NIZAM'S
STATE RAILWAY,
INDIA.

Eight axle boxes were supplied in August, 1930, for a Light Rail Coach. A further order received later.

These boxes are giving every satisfaction.

THE HOFFMANN
ROLLER BEARING AXLE BOX
FOR TAPER SEATING

THE HOFFMANN MFG. CO. LTD.   CHELMSFORD, ESSEX

7

95. In 1897, Guglielmo Marconi established his first factory in Hall Street. This soon became too small, and in 1912 the New Street factory was opened. Marconi found women's nimble fingers ideal for the light assembly work required for many of the components. However, there was little employment elsewhere for females until the start of the First World War. This picture shows women working in the new condensing and mounting shop shortly after it opened.

96. This picture, taken shortly after the opening of the Marconi works in 1912, shows workers emerging from the factory gates and others coming from the direction of Hoffmann's and Harrisons the Malsters, at the end of a long working day.

97. The Marconi drawing office in 1912. It was considerably more basic than those at Crompton Parkinson and Hoffmann's, even allowing for the fact that 40 years separated them.

98. Early in 1922, the Postmaster General granted permission for the Marconi Company to start the first regular radio service. Transmission started in February from the Company's Writtle Laboratories, where the necessary equipment was hastily rigged up in an ex-army hut, shown here. Thus Britain's first radio station, with 2MT – Two Emma Toc – as its call sign, came into existence. From these early beginnings the BBC developed. The hut was later moved and used by a local school but is now preserved by the borough council.

Public Services

99. Decorated for the Harvest Festival, the Methodist church in High Street was built in 1898 to accommodate 500 worshippers on two floors, with a school at the rear. It was demolished in the 1960s to make way for the present ugly multi-storey office block with its ground-floor shops.

100. Chelmsford Corn Exchange was built in 1857 by Fred Chancellor and had an impressive neo-Renaissance frontage facing Tindal Square. This interior view of the Exchange is busy with vendors and purchasers of corn, but it was also used for many other purposes, as diverse as dancing and dog shows.

101. A photograph of Chelmsford livestock market, c.1900, showing cattle and sheep pens. The market transferred in post-war years to a new site in Victoria Road but has subsequently moved to Springfield. The site shown here is now occupied by the multi-storey car-park.

THE AWFUL FATE OF AN INCENDIARY

CONVICT - GAOL

This Engraving represents the Entrance of the County of Essex Convict Gaol—the Place of Execution on the Morning of the 27th of March, 1829, when James Cook, a boy only 16 years of age, suffered for the atrocious crime of setting on fire the premises of Mr. William Green, of Witham, farmer, with whom he lived as Cow Boy.

The Buildings and Stacks, which are represented as burning, furnish a true picture of the lamentable destruction of property occasioned by this wicked boy.

It is a melancholy fact, that there are offenders of the same cast still abroad, who by their conduct, show, that the disgraceful end of Cook has not operated as a sufficient example, to deter them from the commission of the like heinous crime; such, however, may be assured, that justice will ultimately overtake and punish them.

102.   The present gaol at Springfield was erected in 1822 when even minor crimes received very severe sentences. This engraving illustrates the public hanging of a boy of 16 for setting fire to farm buildings in 1829.

103.   Patrol men and their cars outside the Essex County Police headquarters at New Court, Springfield, *c.*1935.

Statistics for the Month of FEBRUARY, 1948.

POLICE DIVISION	Number of Accidents Reported.	Number of persons (excluding children) killed *	Number of persons (excluding children) injured	Number of children killed *	Number of children injured
Braintree ...	49	—	17	—	5
Brentwood ...	70	—	25	—	4
Chelmsford ...	55	1	28	—	1
Clacton	16	—	5	—	2
Epping	21	—	10	—	1
Colchester ...	32	—	9	—	1
Grays	26	—	11	—	4
Romford	68	1	22	—	6
Saffron Walden	22	—	10	—	1
Totals ... ... (at time of going to Press)	359	2	137	—	25

* See below

Comparative figures for FEB., over 3 years are as follows :—
(including Colchester Borough)

	Number of Accidents Reported	Number of persons (excluding children) killed	Number of persons (excluding children) injured	Number of children killed	Number of children injured
1945 ...	311	6	160	—	33
1946 ...	377	3	128	1	32
1947 ...	441	5	122	—	20

FATAL ACCIDENTS

During February two adult pedestrians were killed in road accidents within the Essex Police District.

In the first case, at Chelmsford just after mid-day on the 12th, a man was walking under a narrow railway bridge, with his back to the traffic, on the side of the road where there was no footpath. A lorry being driven through the arch, in the same direction, swerved to avoid an oncoming vehicle and in doing so crushed the pedestrian between the lorry and the bridgework. The man died later in hospital.

The second case occurred at Romford just after 6 p.m. on the 12th, near a junction well lighted by a modern daylight lighting system. It appears that three women were standing in the centre of the road apparently waiting for a motor-cyclist to pass. Suddenly two of the women ran towards the near-side kerb, leaving the third woman alone in the roadway. After hesitating for a few moments this woman then attempted to follow the first two and, as the motor-cycle was almost abreast at the time, ran on to the machine causing it to overturn and drag her along the road. The woman died later in hospital.

These two accidents illustrate the danger of pedestrians walking in the road, especially when doing so with their backs towards the traffic, and the danger of standing about or hesitating when crossing the road.

If it is necessary to walk in the road, walk so as to FACE THE ONCOMING TRAFFIC, and when about to cross over a road WAIT UNTIL IT IS CLEAR AND SAFE TO DO SO, then **walk quickly across by the shortest possible route.**

104. The police have always been concerned about road safety as this leaflet of March 1948 shows. Even then, children accounted for a large proportion of the casualties.

105. Before the war every local council was required to maintain its own fire brigade. The Chelmsford Rural District had fire stations at Great Waltham, Ingatestone and Great Baddow. Here, the coach builders, Munnions, proudly display three new tenders they built for the Council at their Great Baddow works, c.1938.

106. The 1938 volunteer fire crew from the Great Baddow station had very simple but effective fire fighting equipment – though hardly comparable with the high technological approach of their successors, the Essex County Fire and Rescue Service, today.

107. Rainsford House was originally built *c.*1900 as a private house, but from 1924 served as the town's municipal offices. It was demolished in the 1960s to make way for the present Civic Centre.

108. This commemorative plaque was unveiled by the Chairman of Essex County Council, J. H. Burrows J.P. to mark the start of construction on the first stage of County Hall in April 1933.

Hospitals

The Chelmsford Infirmary and Dispensary in London Road was opened by the Countess of Warwick in 1883. Originally it was quite small, being merely a cottage hospital, but it expanded rapidly, with further wards at the rear. Various nearby buildings were taken over. Bellfields, which had been the home of Chelmsford's first mayor, Fred Chancellor, became a convalescent home and Thornwood, a nurses' home. A small isolation hospital was sited in Baddow Road. Chelmsford Hospital was maintained by voluntary subscriptions and public fund-raising activities, such as the massive pre-war week-long Chelmsford Hospital carnival, when nurses and staff constituted the bulk of the helpers. In 1946 the hospital was taken over by the newly formed National Health Service.

In the 1930s the public authorities were making a determined effort to deal with the scourge of tuberculosis. The only treatment available was rest and fresh air. The Essex County Council built a three-storeyed sanatorium at Broomfield with open balconies and wards facing south, in order to provide a bracing but healthy environment. It opened just prior to the war. There was also a small private T.B. hospital, known as Merivale Sanatorium, at Howe Green, Sandon, which took the form of small individual bungalows, set in gardens. In the late 1950s an effective treatment for tuberculosis was found and sanatoria became unnecessary. Broomfield was converted into a general hospital, at first running in tandem with the Chelmsford and Essex Hospital. It has recently been considerably enlarged to become the main district hospital. The original dispensary building at New London Road has been converted into a day health centre and the later extensions removed. Bellfields and Thornwoods have been converted into offices.

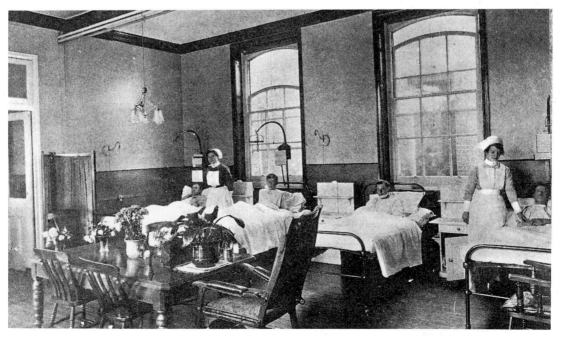

109.   The men's ward at the Chelmsford and Essex Hospital about the turn of the century. The inevitable aspidistra and flowers decorate the sturdy table, which together with the chairs are collector's items today.

St John's Hospital in Wood Street was built during the Second World War on the site of 'Napoleonic' barracks, and consisted of a hutted general hospital and a maternity block. Prior to the war a large mental hospital at Runwell was constructed by the County Boroughs of East and West Ham and Southend to serve patients in the area. It is now administered by the National Health Service. For many years a small leper colony existed at Bicknacre, administered by an Anglican order of nuns and one of only two such hospitals in the United Kingdom.

110.   Broomfield Sanatorium was built in the grounds of Broomfield Court in the late 1930s by the Essex County Council for the treatment of tuberculosis. Sunlight, fresh air and rest, then the only known cures, were the order of the day, so all the wards faced south with open verandahs. Broomfield Court itself became the nurses' home. The hospital has since become a general hospital after major alterations and considerable extensions.

Education

In the Victorian era, churches played a prominent part in the provision of elementary education. The Church of England founded National Schools, whilst Nonconformists ran British Schools like those at New London Road and the Methodist church, High Street. Both were well represented in the town but the situation varied in the villages. In the 19th century at Broomfield there was keen rivalry between church and chapel, whilst the smaller villages were likely to have only a National School. Many of the original buildings still survive in some areas, such as Stock, where the name National School can still be distinguished on the front wall of the school. Church schools were also established at this time at Victoria Road, Cottage Place, The Friars and St John's. The town council began to play a leading role in education. In 1910 it built the Trinity Road school, on the eastern side of the town, providing elementary education for five- to fourteen-year-olds. Kings Road school was built a few years later to serve the western side of the community. The council was also active in the rural district and in 1912 a new school was built at Broomfield to replace the former church school.

By the middle of the 1930s other educational establishments were necessary and on 21 September 1938 Moulsham school was declared open by the then Mayor of Chelmsford, Councillor J. T. Bellamy J.P. It provided places for 250 infants, 300 junior boys, 300 junior girls, 360-80 senior boys and 360-80 senior girls. A similar school, Rainsford, was opened a few months later for senior boys and girls. These two schools and others built in the post-war years became comprehensive when the Essex County Council adopted this form of education, and the school leaving age was raised by stages to 18 years old.

Prior to the passing of the 1944 Education Act only three schools provided secondary education. These were the long established King Edward VI grammar school, the County Girls High School in Broomfield Road, and the Mid-Essex Technical College and School of Art, junior school, in Market Road (now Victoria Road South). The last-mentioned was opened by the Essex County Council in 1935 and superceded a more modest establishment on the same site which had been run by the Borough Council called Chelmsford School of Science and Art. Despite having rapidly established a good reputation, the school did not survive long. In 1975, it was relocated and its name changed before it finally merged with the Broomfield County Secondary school to become the Chelmer Valley High school, one of the district's highly successful comprehensive schools.

111.   The former Roxwell National school, built in 1834 by Thomas William Branston of Skreens, Roxwell. It was able to accommodate up to 170 children in somewhat cramped conditions, with the teacher living in the school house.

112.   (Above right) The former County Technical Laboratories were established in 1893 as the forerunner to Writtle Agricultural College. In 1903 staff and pupils moved to a building in King Edward Avenue, before transferring to Writtle in 1938 and the building was then used by the Essex County Council. It has since been demolished and replaced by an extension to County Hall.

Writtle Agricultural College, formerly known as the Essex Institute of Agriculture, was originally located in King Edward Avenue before it moved to its present site in 1938. H.R.H. Alice, Duchess of Gloucester performed the opening ceremony. Since then it has enhanced its reputation nationally in a wide variety of activities, and increased in size to become one of the finest in the country, with over 1,000 full- and part-time students.

113. Two views of Moulsham Schools in 1938. The top picture shows the junior school on the left and the caretaker's house and infants' school on the right. In the distance is the senior school which also features in the lower picture.

MONDAY	MATHS	HISTORY		DRAMA		MATHS	ENGLISH	LIBRARY
	9·30 & 10·15	10·15 & 11·0	P L A Y T I M E	11·15 & 12·0	D I N N E R	1·45 & 2·30	2·30 & 3·15	3·15 & 4·0
TUESDAY	MATHS	ENGLISH		SCIENCE		MATHS	P.ST.	GARDENING
WEDNSDAY	MATHS	ENGLISH		GAMES		MATHS	MUSIC	ENGLISH
THURSDAY	WOOD AND METAL	WORK		WOOD AND METAL WORK		LITERATURE	ENGLISH	ART AND CRAFT
FRIDAY	TECHNICAL DRAWING	ART AND CRAFT		MUSIC		MATHS	GEOGRAPHY	ENGLISH

114. An 11-year-old pupil's timetable of 1939 for Moulsham senior school. Although the normal school leaving age was then 14, a wide syllabus was followed, which provided a basic education for employment at local factories or, for the more able students, higher education elsewhere.

115. Trinity Road Infant School, 1934. This picture was carefully posed so that these six-year-olds were arranged with a boy and a girl at each bench instead of their normal arrangement of boys on one side of the room and girls on the other.

116. Pupils outside the Chelmsford County High School for Girls, c.1905. Until the Mid-Essex Technical College, Junior School opened in 1936, it was the only school in the district providing secondary education for girls.

117. Practical subjects formed an important part of the curriculum at both Rainsford and Moulsham schools. The picture on the right shows the dressmaking and needlework class at Rainsford school in 1949. Boys were taught woodwork and metalwork.

Transport

Chelmsford had been a highway focal point since early times and was a major coaching stage with roads radiating out to other towns and surrounding villages. The old Roman road to Colchester was an important turnpike, with many inns providing overnight accommodation for coaches, private carriages and gigs. Local produce was also brought into town, either by cart or wagon.

In 1797 the Chelmer and Blackwater Navigation from Heybridge Basin at Maldon to Chelmsford was opened. For 180 years the main wharves at Springfield Basin received a vast array of bulk materials. Although this was destined for the town, substantial quantities were initially hauled away to the surrounding villages. There were also village wharves along the waterway. Coal was of particular importance and was carted to customers as far away as Brentwood. However, with the construction of the railway in 1843 most of this traffic transferred to rail. Although the line cuts diagonally through the district, only the station at Chelmsford was provided. A small passenger station was built on the edge of town together with a goods yard (later much enlarged). The passenger station was rebuilt in the late 1980s.

Although there were a few horse buses, the first real bus service – with routes to and from Danbury, Broomfield and Writtle – was started by the Great Eastern Railway Company in 1905 as feeders to the trains. The National Steam Car Company later developed a more comprehensive service which operated from a bus station in Duke Street. There were also several smaller companies such as Hicks Bros. Ltd., which ran services from a small bus station in Park Road to Broomfield and Braintree, and Moores of Kelvedon which operated between Colchester and Ashdown to Danbury. The post-war Labour government nationalised buses, and these smaller companies were taken over by the Eastern National Bus Company Ltd., the National's successor.

118.   Springfield Basin, the head of the Chelmer and Blackwater Navigation, *c*.1930, where barges carrying a variety of cargoes from Heybridge Basin once unloaded.

119. One of the last horse-drawn lighters approaches Springfield Basin laden with timber for Brown & Son Ltd., *c.*1950. Brown's continued to work the canal commercially for a further 20 years using motor barges.

120. The canal between Chelmsford and the sea has 13 locks, each with two pairs of gates which are renewed at regular intervals and are hand crafted. This photograph was taken at Paper Mill Lock, Little Baddow in 1950.

121.   Chelmsford Railway Station, *c.*1910. The *Saracen's Head* horse-drawn omnibus awaits the hotel guests, whilst a service bus is also on-hand for passengers.

122. One of the Stratford-built fleet of Great Eastern Railway buses at its terminus at Great Waltham. The buses were withdrawn in 1913, when taken over by the National, who then used steam powered buses.

123. A Guys double-decker Eastern National bus arrives from Maldon, c.1950.

124.   Slewed across Victoria Road and apparently oblivious of any other traffic, Hicks Brothers proudly display their new charabanc, c.1930.

125.   In 1925 Ernest Lodge, a Writtle baker, was one of the first tradesmen in the village to own a motor vehicle.

126. Rose Brothers' taxis in the early 1930s. For many years, the two brothers ran a taxi service, as well as Primrose coaches, taking bookings via a tiny shop in Duke Street.

127. A line of vehicles in Navigation Road, c.1920, owned by Brown & Son Ltd., timber merchants.

128. Duke Street, 1929. The right-hand side is virtually unchanged but the bus station has since been greatly enlarged and rebuilt.

129. Thomas Clarkson, the bus manufacturer (sitting on the running board) with his family and Model T Ford outside their house at Runsell Green, 1912.

130.   Motoring was the prerogative of the middle and upper classes until the second half of the present century. At Hill House, Broomfield, the family of John Smith gather around their open tourer, *c.*1945.

Should be 1935?

Wartime

Chelmsford played its full part in both the world wars. During the First World War the town's main activity was to provide munitions and armaments. Most men of military age either volunteered or were called up for service whilst the women of Chelmsford entered the factories and the workplace for the first time. Soldiers were stationed in and around the area, as large numbers of troops were retained in the country ready to foil any possible invasion of eastern England. Camps were established in various places and troops were billeted in private houses, public houses or any structure which could be made habitable. Oaklands House, now Chelmsford Museum, was used as a military hospital with temporary hutted wards in the grounds. Hylands Park was used by the army and a primitive airfield existed at Springfield on land now occupied by the Allied Housing Estate. At Galleywood, the racecourse grandstand was pressed into service by an artillery regiment as a temporary barracks and as a quartermaster's stores. In 1915, Chelmsford prison was taken over by the War Department for four years, and was used partly as a soldiers' detention centre and partly as a German prisoner-of-war camp.

The start of the Second World War on 3 September 1939 brought a whole new way of life to Chelmsford. A blackout was immediately enforced and the street lights turned off. Most households hurriedly purchased heavy curtains or constructed removable blackout frames to cover the windows. Windows were pasted with netting, or criss-crossed with sticky paper to prevent flying glass. Food rationing was introduced and gas masks issued.

Chelmsford was initially classified as a reception area for children evacuated from London, as it was correctly foreseen that the capital would be the subject of an unremitting bombing campaign. Complete schools were moved to the district. At Moulsham, schools played host to Leyton's Cann Hall school, and the Mid-Essex Technical College provided accommodation for the West Ham Technical College. However, after a few months it was apparent that Chelmsford, although comparatively small, was a worthwhile target, with its important ball bearing, radio and electrical factories contributing to wartime production. The evacuees were moved further away, but not before the first bombs had been dropped on the town. On 13 October 1940 a bomb tragically killed the Mayor, Alderman John Thompson and his entire family, who were living in a large house in New London Road.

Air activity became frequent and the first plane to be brought down in the Battle of Britain crashed in the grounds of Bishops Court in Springfield Road. Most of the crew were killed although one was lucky enough to parachute to safety near Margaretting. Shortly afterwards, a Spitfire dived into the side of a house in New London Road, killing the pilot.

In the early stages of the war Chelmsford was virtually undefended, apart from a few mounted Lewis guns and some searchlights, but this soon changed when a number of prefabricated steel towers, approximately 30 ft. high, were built at various sites on which Bofors anti-aircraft guns were mounted. One was sited on vacant land in Sandford Road and another at Boarded Barnes A concrete version, which survived until the 1970s, was sited on allotments at the rear of the former R.H.P. factory. Another gun was mounted on the roof of the egg factory in Victoria Road and others were moved continuously around the streets of Chelmsford. Simultaneously,

31 barrage balloons were stationed in and around the town in order to discourage aircraft passing beneath them and hitting the cables. Subsequent defences included rocket guns manned by the Home Guard at the recreation ground, and batteries of 3.7 and 4.5 anti-aircraft guns at various locations, including Sandon (where Area Command was based) and Rettendon.

In an attempt to foil German raiders a dummy town was built close to the river near Little Baddow. It was hoped that the German planes would use the river to fly a path to Chelmsford and inadvertently drop their bombs short of the town.

On 15 April and 14 May 1943 the town suffered concentrated raids, with the Germans announcing that Chelmsford was the night's prime target. Considerable damage was inflicted on the town especially when a drill hall in Market Road, used as an ammunitions dump, was hit by an incendiary bomb. Chelmsford was also attacked by Doodlebugs (V1s), one of which destroyed the swimming pool. Thankfully this occurred early one morning, before it had opened; otherwise many people – mainly children – would have been killed or seriously injured, including the writer. In 1944, Hitler's second secret weapon, the V2 rockets, began falling haphazardly throughtout the whole area, without warning, by day and night. Many fell harmlessly in the surrounding fields and woods but unfortunately two local factories were hit, killing and injuring many workers.

In 1940, after the fall of France, when Britain was threatened with invasion, various measures were established to aid the country's defence. A citizens' army was created. They were originally called the Local Defence Volunteers but this quickly changed and they became known as the Home Guard. Initially, they were armed only with home-made weapons such as pikes, made from knives fixed to the end of broom-sticks, but as the war progressed they were more suitably equipped. In the Chelmsford area, their main task, apart from manning the rockets, was to delay any advancing troops and destroy anything which might aid the enemy, including roads and bridges. Spigot mortar emplacements were set up at strategic places.

A line of defences was built along the upper Chelmer through Great and Little Waltham, Broomfield, Springfield, Sandon and to the main road towards Rettendon. It consisted of a series of concrete pill-boxes and gun emplacements, together with concrete blocks, anti-tank ditches and barbed wire emplacements. Minor lanes along the route were made ready to be blocked. After the war, the ditches were filled in and the land turned over to agriculture, but the pill-boxes still remain.

With the fortunes of war turning in favour of the Allies, prisoners of war arrived in Britain. Camps for German prisoners of war were established next to Chelmer Road, on what is now Coronation Park and near Second Avenue. There was an Italian P.O.W. camp near Little Baddow. Army camps existed in various places including Bicknacre and Roxwell.

A large military airfield was hurriedly constructed at Boreham, displacing fields, orchards and woodlands. There the United States Army Airforce established a base and flew sorties over occupied Europe, in partnership with the R.A.F., and caused considerable damage to the enemy, but not without suffering heavy losses them-selves. Among the planes stationed at Boreham were B26's, a type of fighter bomber, known as Marauders. In Chelmsford, the Americans took over the *Saracens Head Hotel* as a leave hostel, and the local pubs, cinemas and dance halls greatly benefited from their custom. As elsewhere, they were very popular with the local girls.

With the end of the war, Boreham airfield, like so many military bases, fell into disuse. For some time the perimeter track was used as a testing ground for Ford cars and there were even one or two pop concerts held there. Many of the former airmen's huts became occupied by squatters, who were eventually allocated council houses elsewhere. Today, only the concrete runways remain.

131. During the First World War the Corn Exchange was pressed into service as a recreation centre for off-duty soldiers. In the Second World War, it was again popular with the forces as a dance hall.

132. Broomfield camp in 1915, and life under canvas was not all fun, as these glum-looking privates would probably testify.

133. During the First World War large numbers of troops were billeted in and around the town. Here, is a group gathered outside the *Compasses* public house in Broomfield Road, *c*.1915, together with some of the locals.

134. Most commodities in the 1940s - food, clothes and fuel - were in short supply and the public were encouraged to be economical.

Your blackout—is it all that it should be? Long spells of immunity from serious air raids are apt to breed slackness and a sort of false bravado which is all too often only thinly disguised laziness. The nuisance raider who has lost his way and is anxious to get home before a night fighter catches him, needs little excuse for unloading his bombs. Your poor blackout may provide him with all the excuse he wants. It is no solace to you to hear (if you are still alive to hear anything) your modest dwelling subsequently described by Lord Haw-Haw as an "important military objective."

YOUR MONEY

Don't keep any more money in the house than necessary for day-to-day expenses. There will be no compensation for cash or notes destroyed by enemy action.

The Navy, the Army, the Air Force, the Defence Services and the workers everywhere—in factory and mine, in the civil and municipal services, whether producing food or munitions, all know that their work is vital. But it is no good being prepared to put all your energy into your job if there is no money to supply you with the essentials for life and work. Without money we are unable to fight!

135. Throughout the Second World War, Chelmsford, like much of Britain, came under constant threat of air attack and a strict blackout was enforced. Reminders appeared in the press and Air Raid Wardens patrolled at night.

136 & 137. Chelmsford suffered concentrated air raids on 15 April and 14 May 1943. The first was mainly a firebomb attack whilst the second raid destroyed and damaged many buildings. The picture above shows the remains of Hawkes confectionery shop on the corner of Victoria Road and Duke Street, whilst the picture below shows ruined houses in Park Avenue, which were subsequently rebuilt.

CHELMSFORD
BOROUGH AND RURAL DISTRICT
WAR-SHIP WEEK
1942

FEBRUARY 14——FEBRUARY 21

NATIONAL SAVINGS MOVEMENT
PATRON : HIS MAJESTY THE KING.

WARSHIP WEEK COMMITTEE.

CHAIRMAN : His Worship the Mayor, Sidney C. Taylor, Esq., J.P.
VICE-CHAIRMAN : Chairman Rural District Council : A. G Falkner, Esq., J.P.
HON. TREASURER : A. E. Bandey, Esq., National Provincial Bank, Ltd.
HON. SECRETARY : Fred. R. Kearsley, Esq., 17 London Road, Chelmsford.

GENERAL COMMITTEE :

F. H. Andrew, Esq.	F. G. Elkington, Esq.	C. E. Rickard, Esq.
A. E. Bandey, Esq.	B. L. Humphrys, Esq.	N. Squier, Esq.
A. H. Beeton, Esq.	F. Hutchinson, Esq.	A. Sykes, Esq.
L. G. Bird, Esq.	H. F. Pash, Esq.	R. J. Thompson, Esq.
P. Butchard, Esq.	E. C. Pollard, Esq.	N. G. Treloar, Esq.
M. C. Dewdney, Esq.	C. Plumtree, Esq.	

INVESTMENTS COMMITTEE : Chairman : L. Grafton Bird, Esq.
PUBLICITY COMMITTEE : Chairman : R. J. Thompson, Esq.
RETURNING OFFICER : E. C. Pollard, Esq., Barclays Bank, Ltd.
ACTIVITIES COMMITTEE : Hon. Secretary : A. H. Beeton, Esq.

OUR AIM :

Not less than £240,000 to be invested in National Funds to pay for two Corvettes. If we succeed we have been informed that Chelmsford Borough and Rural District will be allowed to adopt—

H.M.S. " CORIANDER "
and
H.M.S. " CYCLAMEN "

INVEST IN VICTORY

---

138.   National Savings were encouraged to finance the war effort with special events like Salute the Soldier, Wings for Victory, and Warship Week. For the latter, a target of £240,000 was set, which in those days was sufficient to buy two corvettes. The week included a series of promotional activities and social events such as dances, film shows, whist drives, ballet, concerts and football matches, but the highlight was a parade of Canadian and Indian soldiers marching through the town.

CHELMSFORD'S RECORD IN NATIONAL SAVINGS

I⊤ was in June, 1916, that Miss Bancroft, of the Chelmsford High School for Girls, started a National Savings Group, closely followed by the Essex County Council under Mr. A. V. Phillips. The late Alderman Thompson called a further meeting in December, 1916, when a National Savings Committee was formed with Mr. Seager as secretary. The Movement grew very rapidly in Chelmsford, and at the close of the Great War was extremely flourishing.

After the War the late Alderman Thompson still took a very keen interest in the movement and the secretary, Mr. W. F. Arlidge, was a most capable secretary until his death in 1927. Mr. R. W. Blyth then became hon. secretary until 1935. when Mr. W. G. Staines took over the office.

It is interesting to note that the Essex County Council Group celebrated its Silver Jubilee last year, and still has the same secretary, Mr. A. V. Phillips.

In 1939 the late Alderman Thompson called a Town Meeting, when it was decided to separate the Borough from the Rural District, and Mr. F. R. Kearsley became the hon. secretary of the Chelmsford Borough, and Mr. W. G Staines of the Rural District. Several special weeks have been held, and although the amount aimed at in War Weapons Week was not obtained it was only £11,000 below the Target. The amount subscribed in Chelmsford and the Rural District since the commencement of this War is over £1,250,000 and the number of Groups has increased by over 200 in the Borough alone—a very satisfactory record.

The Committee are more than anxious that in the coming Warship Week we shall not only obtain our Target to pay for H.M.S. " Coriander " and H.M.S. " Cyclamen," but enough money to provide a third.

139 & 140. The Germans considered Chelmsford a prime target as Hoffmann's, Marconi's and Crompton's were all involved in important war work. The photograph on the right shows a girl winding a small transformer at Marconi's factory, New Street, in the early 1940s, whilst the picture below shows workers at the same factory, assembling radio equipment.

141. Although initially almost undefended, Chelmsford's air defences eventually included rockets, guns, light and heavy anti-aircraft guns and barrage balloons, all of which were deployed in and around the town. A battery of rocket launchers was installed in the Recreation Ground, now Central Park, and operated by the Home Guard, together with ammunition dumps and shelters. A number of aircraft hits were claimed, one of which came down in flames at Great Leighs.

142. This concrete Flack tower, built about 1942, was on allotments at the rear of Hoffmann's Works, with a Bofors anti-aircraft gun stationed on the deck, and ammunition stores below. The tower was demolished in the early 1980s to make way for the Chelmer Valley Road. Similar towers, made of prefabricated steel, were sited elsewhere.

143.   From 1942 to the end of the War, 64 twin rocket projectors were stationed in the Recreation Ground (now Central Park). In this picture, four gunners of the 211(101 Essex Home Guard) 'Z' A.A. Battery R. A. stand by one of their projectors. Two gunners display a pair of the six-foot long rockets about to be launched which would explode at a predetermined height.

144. David Smith, pictured above left in full sergeant's uniform and carrying a .303 rifle and respirator. He was a well-known Essex author, broadcaster and farmer, and served in the Broomfield Company of the Home Guard, firstly as a sergeant and later as an officer.

145. An aircraft spotter on the roof of Marconi House, New Street. Although advance warning of enemy bombers was provided via Radar and the Royal Observer Corps, they gave vital 'on the spot' information.

146. Thirty-one R.A.F. barrage balloons were deployed in and around the town with moorings on various sites. These remains of an airmen's Nissen hut next to the Wood Street roundabout were photographed in 1981, just prior to the site's development.

Events

147.   A most destructive flood occurred in July 1888, when the centre of the town was inundated. There were similar floods in 1947 and 1958 but subsequent river works have prevented reoccurrence.

148. In its heyday, the annual Chelmsford hospital carnival procession featured many ingenious floats. Apprentices from the three major firms vied to display the most original exhibit. In 1927, the Great War was still fresh in the memory and the Crompton apprentices were able to parade this realistic looking tank, built around a works vehicle.

149. The picture below shows, King George V inspecting troops of the South Midland Division at Hylands Park, 14 October 1914.

150. A large group in front of the conduit at the Springfield Road junction, *c.*1915, flanked by two of Clarkson's steam buses.

151. This aerial picture shows the paddock area and the grandstand at Galleywood Racecourse, during what was undoubtedly one of its last events, in the mid-1930s. Sadly, the grandstand has since been demolished and the paddock area is now a Council maintenance yard.

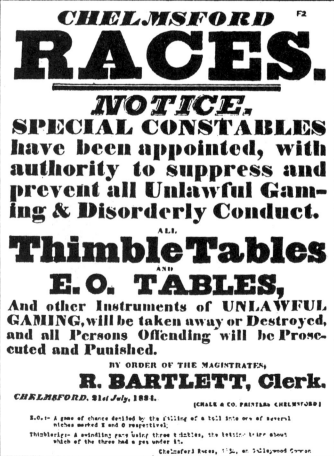

CHELMSFORD F2
RACES.

NOTICE.
SPECIAL CONSTABLES
have been appointed, with authority to suppress and prevent all Unlawful Gaming & Disorderly Conduct.

ALL

Thimble Tables
AND
E. O. TABLES,
And other Instruments of UNLAWFUL GAMING, will be taken away or Destroyed, and all Persons Offending will be Prosecuted and Punished.

BY ORDER OF THE MAGISTRATES,
R. BARTLETT, Clerk.
CHELMSFORD, 21st July, 1884.

[CHALK & CO. PRINTERS CHELMSFORD]

E.O.:- A game of chance decided by the falling of a ball into one of several niches marked E and O respectively.

Thimblerig:- A swindling game using three thimbles, the betting being about which of the three had a pea under it.

Chelmsford Races, 1884, on Galleywood Common

152. Although the races were enjoyed by many law abiding citizens, there was undoubtedly an unruly element, as this notice implies, c.1890.

153. Phyllis Holberton, Chelmsford's first Carnival Queen, presents a prize at the 1931 hospital carnival in the Recreation Ground (now Central Park). Miss Holberton later owned a successful salon in Moulsham Street.

154. At the age of 21, Phyllis Holberton was the first ever Chelmsford Hospital Carnival Queen in 1931.

155 & 156. Colonel J. R. Macnamara, the standing Member of Parliament for the Chelmsford Constituency, died on active service and a by-election was held in April 1945, one of the few called in the war. Ernest Millington *(above right)* was elected for the Common Wealth Party and a few months later was again elected at the General Election before joining the Labour Party. The Conservative and National Candidate Flight Lieutenant Brian Cook *(above left)* was heavily defeated.

157. This clever cartoon, which appeared in the now defunct newspaper, the *Chelmsford Clarion*, lampoons the council elections of 1 November 1946.

158 & 159.   The town centre was lavishly decorated with flags and bunting for the coronation of Queen Elizabeth II in June 1953. The occasion was celebrated in style with a series of special events, including a procession through the town together with a fête and fair in the Recreation Ground, now Central Park.

160. A 1930s Primrose coach, outside the firm's booking office in Duke Street, prior to a bachelors' outing.

TO-MORROW WEEK AT CHELMSFORD

SATURDAY, MARCH 20.

County Welcome & Presentation

Of SILVER DRUMS

To the 1st Batt. of The Essex Regiment

CHELMSFORD FOOTBALL FIELD in New Writtle Street.

OUTLINE OF THE PROGRAMME

2. 0.—Ground Opens and Band Plays.
2.15.—Ex-members 1st and 2nd Battalions march off from Market Road.
2.20.—Battalion arrives at Railway Station.
2.30.—Battalion marches off for the Football Field.
2.40.—The British Legion march off from the Station for the Field.
3. 0.—The Lord-Lieutenant's Procession leaves The Elms.

The Inspection Presentation, and Trooping of the Colour will follow.

And then a Triumphal March of the Battalion through the Streets.

Full details, times, description, etc., in the SPECIAL

SOUVENIR ILLUSTRATED PROGRAMME

Of twenty pages, on sale from Monday Next. Sixpence.

IMPORTANT NOTICE.— No Seats in the Grand Stand can be Reserved after 2.45 p.m.

Members of the British Legion are asked to parade at the Drill Hall, Chelmsford, at 1.45 p.m., on Saturday, March 20th. Members of the Chelmsford Branch will be instructed at the General Meeting on Monday, the 15th. Members of any other Branches must notify their intention of attending to Col. Barrington C. Wells, D.S.O., 26 Duke Street, not later than Wednesday morning, March 17th.

J. O. THOMPSON, Chairman.
F. U. BRADBRIDGE, Hon. Sec., Essex County Committee.
FRED. SPALDING, Chairman and Hon. Sec., Borough Committee.

161. In recognition of their outstanding service in France and Palestine 1914-18, the 1st Battalion of the Essex Regiment were ceremonially presented with new silver drums at the Football Ground in New Writtle Street, March 1926.

162. In pre-war and early post-war years, dances were popular weekend events. In addition to the Corn Exchange and the Shire Hall, Cannon's Restaurant in Duke Street was also a popular venue.

The Second Annual Dance of "The Pirates Cricket Club" will be held on Friday 12th November, 1937, from 9 p.m. to 1 a.m. at

CANNON'S RESTAURANT, CHELMSFORD.

Walking the plank on this auspicious occasion will be to the accompaniment of "BARNEY'S" band—the best. It is to be regretted that there will also be a licensed BAR. Further there will be provided an excellent SUPPER.

We have no hesitation in asking you to come (with a large party please) because we sincerely hope you will have a great time. We shall do our best to see that you do.

THE PIRATES.

P.S. We forgot to mention that tickets price 5/- can be obtained in advance from the Hon. Secretary, A. G. Wilks, Mount Cottage, Widford, Chelmsford, or any member of the Committee. They will also be available at the door.

163. A swimming gala in progress. The Chelmsford pool was normally open from 1 May to 31 September each year. It was built in 1906 on land next to the present leisure centre and used filtered water obtained from the adjacent river. It was replaced by the present outdoor pool in the 1980s.

164. The Chelmsford Boating Club, now Chelmsford Canoe Club, began in 1946, and was instrumental in bringing the sport of canoeing to the area. For many years as part of Chelmsford carnival they held a canoe regatta in Central Park lake. This photograph, c.1950, captures a moment in the mixed double event when Charmaine Closs and David Eade went into the lead.

165. Ever since it was opened in 1797, the Company of Proprietors of the Chelmer and Blackwater Navigation have made an annual inspection of their canal between Chelmsford and Heybridge Basin. Chelmsford Duke, led by Fred Hoy, is seen towing the lighter out of Sandford Lock *c.*1955, one of the last times a horse-drawn working boat was used. Today, the annual inspection is carried out from a motor boat.

166. Before the advent of radio and television the circus and fairs were eagerly awaited events. In April 1932, Bertram Mill's marquee was erected at the junction of Writtle Road and New London Road. Acrobats, jugglers, clowns, together with lions, tigers, elephants, horses and ponies were all to be seen for only 1s. 3d. (six pence).

People

167. The Clarkson family at their home at Runsell Green in 1912: from left to right – Margaret, Alec, Mrs. Lottie Clarkson, Thomas Clarkson, .. All worked at Thomas Clarkson's Bus Works at Queens Street. Alec Clarkson later went to the Isle of Wight to work on boatbuilding before emigrating to America.

168. David Smith, of Hill House, Broomfield, a local author, broadcaster and farmer in the early post-war years (*see* no. 144).

169. A West Hanningfield farm worker in the typical hard wearing clothes of the time, c.1920.

170. Fire is an ever present hazard at factories, and Hoffmann's from their early days maintained their own permanent fire brigade. This 1950 photograph of the brigade includes, front centre, J. W. Garton, the managing director, and next to him the works manager, Sidney Gregory.

171 & 172. Chelmsford Hockey Club, established in 1898, is one of the oldest clubs in the country. Its first pitch was at Vicarage Lane, Chelmsford, on land farmed by Herbert Marriage. The club was always able to field teams for Ladies', Men's and Mixed events, as can be seen in the photograph below from 1903. Today, the Club plays at Chelmer Park.

173.   In 1934, a children's party was held at a house in Victoria Road, followed by games in Tunman Mead, an attractive and popular open space next to the River Chelmer, now part of the Victoria Road car-park. Among those present were Mary Rowe, John Bausor, John Marriage, Brian Fisher, Jean Alison and Neville Metcalfe.

174.   The Chelmsford and East Essex Musical Competition held in May 1909 at the old Corn Exchange in Tindal Square. The building was an ideal venue for many important community events complementing its main use as an agricultural centre. Unfortunately this extremely functional and attractive building was demolished to make way for the present shopping precinct, which in hindsight seems a rather bad planning decision.

175. Chelmsford has always supported a wealth of musical and choral groups. This group photograph is of the Chelmsford Singers in 1929.

176. Members of the Chelmsford Athletic Club in 1935 with His Worship the Mayor, Alderman Taylor, and Mr. Arthur Beeton, the Club's Hon. Secretary (centre).

177. Gwen Herbert of the Chelmsford City Girls football team on the field during a match with London Ladies on 25 January 1951. Chelmsford lost 2 - 3.

178. In the early post-war years all-girl football was popular. Chelmsford City Girls team, with a home ground at Lionmede, was one of the most successful. This picture taken in 1951 shows Gwen Herbert (left) in action against a member of the opposing team.

179.   Air Raid Wardens from the Lionmede Post in 1943. Mr. William Richards (centre, bottom line) was Chief Warden. Two wardens took turns to be on duty each night and were required to deal with any emergencies in their area until help arrived. The post is now a groundsman's store.

180.   A group picture of 'A' Platoon, D Company, 6th Essex Battalion, Home Guard under the command of Lt. C. Barnard (seated centre). The men were recruited and based in the Springfield Hill area of Chelmsford and, had the Germans invaded, one of their duties was to blow up the Esso petrol depot in Victoria Road.

181. Members of the Chelmsford Boating Club (now Chelmsford Canoe Club) with their two double-seater racing canoes after a successful race on the Thames, *c*.1950. Left to right, Tony Mott, Graham Slater, John Marriage, and Charles Price.

Bibliography

'Broomfield Parish Magazine', various issues, 1976-86
*Broomfield: The Official Guide, c.*1950
Chelmsford Borough Council, *Hylands – An Architectural History,* 1988
Chelmsford Centenary Yearbook, 1988
Chelmsford Citizens Handbook, 1943
Chelsmford Official Handbook, 9th ed., 1946
Chelmsford Rural District, *Official Guide,* 1955
Chelmsford Weekly News, various issues
Crawley, R. J., et al., *The Years Between, 1909 to 1929,* 1979
Essex Chronicle, various issues
Essex Countryside, various issues
Grieve, Hilda, *The Sleepers and the Shadows,* 1988
Kelly's Directory of Chelmsford, 1948
Marconi, *A War Record 1939-45,* 1955
Marconi Radar, *Chelmsford News and Views,* April 1985
Marden, P. and Trevor, B., *The Writtle We've Loved,* 1985
Marriage, John, *Chelmsford: A Pictorial History,* 1982
Newton, K. C., *The Manor of Writtle,* 1970
Pevsner, Nikolaus, *The Buildings of England – Essex,* 1954
Roxwell, *A Short Pictorial Record of the Village,* 1985
White, William, *History of the County of Essex,* 1848
Wickenden, Nick, *Caesaromagus – a history and description of Roman Chelmsford,* 1990